Grouping Words

Sentences

Anita Ganeri

KT-574-777

www.raintreepublishers.co.uk
Visit our website to find out
more information about
Raintree books.

To order:
☎ Phone 0845 6044371
📄 Fax +44 (0) 1865 312263
✉ Email myorders@raintreepublishers.co.uk

Customers from outside the UK please telephone +44 1865 312262

Raintree is an imprint of Capstone Global Library Limited,
a company incorporated in England and Wales having its
registered office at 7 Pilgrim Street, London, EC4V 6LB
– Registered company number: 6695582

Edited by Daniel Nunn, Rebecca Rissman, and Sian Smith
Designed by Joanna Hinton-Malivoire
Picture research by Tracy Cummins
Original illustrations © Capstone Global Library
Illustrated by Joanna Hinton-Malivoire
Production by Eirian Griffiths
Originated by Capstone Global Library Ltd
Printed in China

ISBN 978 1 406 23242 4 (hardback)
15 14 13 12 11
10 9 8 7 6 5 4 3 2 1

ISBN 978 1 406 23249 3 (paperback)
16 15 14 13 12
10 9 8 7 6 5 4 3 2 1

British Library Cataloguing in Publication Data
Ganeri, Anita, 1961-
Grouping words: sentences. (Getting to grips with
grammar)
425-dc22
A full catalogue record for this book is available from the
British Library.

Acknowledgements
We would like to thank the following for permission to reproduce
photographs and artworks: Dreamstime.com p.16 © Viorel
Sima; Shutterstock pp.5 (© AnetaPics), 7 (© Cory Thoman), 8 (©
Tony Oshlick), 9 (© Kirill Vorobyev), 11 (© Susan McKenzie), 12 (Eric
Isselée), 13 (© Johan Swanepoel), 17 (© sunsetman), 18 (© Davi
Sales Batista), 19 (© Don Purcell), 21 (© Brocreative), 23 (© Supri
Suharjoto), 24 (© DM7), 26 (© majeczka), 27 (© infografick), 28 (©
Laurie Barr), 29 (© anyaivanova), 30 (© Maxim Slugin).

Every effort has been made to contact copyright holders
of material reproduced in this book. Any omissions will
be rectified in subsequent printings if notice is given to the
publisher.

Contents

Some words are shown in bold, **like this**.
You can find them in the glossary on page 31.

What is grammar?

Grammar is a set of rules that helps you to write and speak a language. Grammar is important because it helps people to understand each other.

in nest. an egg laid its bird The

Without grammar, this sentence doesn't make sense.

This book is about **sentences**.
A sentence is a group of words.
Grammar helps you put the words in
the right order so that they make sense.

The bird laid an egg in its nest.

Grammar turns the
jumbled-up words
into a sentence.

What is a sentence?

A **sentence** begins with a **capital letter**. It ends with a **full stop** or another type of **punctuation mark**.

The dog is chasing a ball.

This sentence starts with a capital 'T' and ends with a full stop.

A sentence must also have a **verb** (a doing word) and it must make sense on its own. Look at the examples below.

I got a.

This is not a sentence. It doesn't make sense on its own.

I got a new bike.

This is a sentence. It makes sense on its own.

Make a sentence

On these two pages, there are some groups of words that are jumbled up. Can you turn them into **sentences**?

animals lots are There zoo. in the of

The monkeys. zookeeper fed the

The correct answers are: There are lots of animals in the zoo. The zookeeper fed the monkeys.

Remember that a sentence starts with a **capital letter** and ends with a **punctuation mark**. It must make sense on its own. Here are two more examples for you to try.

party. I to went birthday a

ice cream. jelly and ate lots I of

The correct answers are: I went to a birthday party. I ate lots of jelly and ice cream.

9

Statements

There are different types of **sentences**. They do different jobs. A statement is a sentence that simply tells you something.

The monster was big and scary.

This sentence is a statement.

Today, it is raining.

In this statement, 'it is raining' is a fact.

In writing, you use statements to tell your readers about facts. Statements always end with a **full stop**.

Questions

A question is a **sentence** that asks for an answer. The sentence below is an example of a question.

This is a question. The answer might be 'yes' or 'no'.

Do you want to play football?

A question begins with a **capital letter**.
It ends with a **question mark** instead of
a **full stop**.

> **Why do I need a haircut?**

> This is a question.
> It has a question
> mark at the end.

Exclamations

An exclamation is a **sentence** that says something strongly or with feeling. It can also show surprise.

This is an exclamation. It shows that the person writing feels strongly about chocolate.

I hate chocolate!

There is a dinosaur in the park!

This is an exclamation. It has an exclamation mark at the end.

An exclamation begins with a **capital letter**. It ends with an **exclamation mark** instead of a **full stop**.

Commands

A command is when you tell someone to do something. You give someone an order.

This is a command. You are giving an order.

Clean your teeth properly.

A command usually starts with a **verb**.
You sometimes put an **exclamation mark** at the end.

Don't eat all the biscuits!

This is a command.
It has an exclamation mark at the end.

Simple sentences

A simple **sentence** has two parts. The first part is the subject. This is the person or thing that the sentence is about.

Holly built a sandcastle.

'Holly' is the subject. The sentence is about her.

The second part of a sentence is what is written or said about the subject. It always has a **verb** in it.

The fish swim in the sea.

The second part of this sentence is 'swim in the sea'. 'Swim' is the verb.

Adding other words

You can make your **sentences** more interesting by adding some **adjectives**. Adjectives are words that describe **nouns** (naming words).

'Enormous' is an adjective. It describes 'sandcastle', which is a noun.

Holly built an enormous sandcastle.

The fish swim slowly in the sea.

'Slowly' is an adverb. It describes 'swims', which is a verb.

You could also try adding **adverbs** to your sentences. Adverbs are words that describe **verbs** (doing words).

Joining sentences

Lots of short **sentences** can be difficult to read. Try joining sentences together. This will help your writing or speech to flow better.

> **I like playing tennis. My sister likes playing football.**

Here are two short sentences. They do not flow very well.

You use **conjunctions** to join sentences together. A conjunction is a joining word, such as 'and', 'but', 'when', or 'because'.

'But' is a conjunction. It joins the two sentences together.

I like playing tennis, but my sister likes playing football.

Phrases

You can make your **sentences** longer by adding **phrases**. A phrase is a group of words. It does not have a **verb** and is not a sentence.

'Across the field' is a phrase.

The horse ran across the field.

Phrases also help to make sentences sound more interesting. You can use them instead of simple **nouns**.

The big, green crocodile **had sharp teeth.**

You add 'big' and 'green' to 'crocodile' to make a phrase.

Clauses

You can also add **clauses** to your **sentences**. A clause is a group of words that *does* have a **verb**.

I ate six cakes because I was hungry.

'Because I was hungry' is a clause and 'was' is the verb used.

The sentence below is made up of two clauses. Each clause has a verb. Each clause works on its own as a simple sentence.

Both of these clauses work on their own.
Joe walked to school.
Sophie rode her bike.

Joe walked to school, but Sophie rode her bike.

Paragraphs

A **paragraph** is a group of **sentences**. The sentences are all about the same thing. Putting your sentences into paragraphs makes your writing easier to read.

Once there was a fierce dragon. It lived in a dark cave under the ground. It guarded a big treasure chest.

This paragraph has three sentences.

Once there was a fierce dragon. It lived in a dark cave under the ground. It guarded a big treasure chest.

The dragon liked breathing fire so it didn't have many friends. Sometimes, it felt very lonely.

The new paragraph starts a little way in from the edge.

In a new paragraph, start the first line a little way in from the edge of the page. This makes it easier to see where the new paragraph begins.

Possible answers

The cow is eating leaves. The brown cow is eating dandelion leaves. The cow ate leaves while the other cows watched. The cow filled its mouth with leaves, under a cloudy sky. Three cows looked at the camera, while the photographer took their picture.

How many **sentences** can you use to describe what is happening here?

Using sentences

Glossary

adjective describing word that tells you more about a noun

adverb describing word that tells you more about a verb

capital letter upper-case letter, such as A, B, C, D, E

clause group of words that does have a verb

conjunction word that joins sentences together

exclamation mark mark at the end of a sentence to show a strong feeling

full stop mark that shows the end of a sentence

grammar a set of rules that helps you to speak or write clearly

noun a naming word

question mark mark at the end of a sentence to show a question

paragraph group of sentences

phrase group of words that does not have a verb

punctuation mark mark used in writing to make the meaning clear

sentence group of words that make sense on their own

verb a doing or action word

Find out more

Books

Go Further with Grammar, Ruth Thomson (Belitha Press, 2004)

Grammar and Punctuation for School (Homework Helpers), Ladybird
(Ladybird Books, 2009)

Grammar Ray series, Andrew Carter (Evans Brothers, 2009)

Websites

www.bbc.co.uk/schools/ks1bitesize/literacy/sentences/index.shtml
Arrange words in the correct order to make sentences.

**www.bbc.co.uk/skillswise/words/grammar/sentencebasics/
whatisasentence/game.shtml**
Can you recognize a sentence? Use these games to test yourself.

Index